JONATHAN HARVEY

God is our Refuge

(Psalm 46)

for SATB and Organ

God is our Refuge was commissioned by the University of Sussex
to celebrate the University's Silver Jubilee in 1986.
The first performance was given at Chichester Cathedral
on 5th June 1986

FABER MUSIC
London

In Celebration of the Silver Jubilee of The University of Sussex (1986)

GOD IS OUR REFUGE

for SATB and Organ

(Words from Psalm 46)

Jonathan Harvey

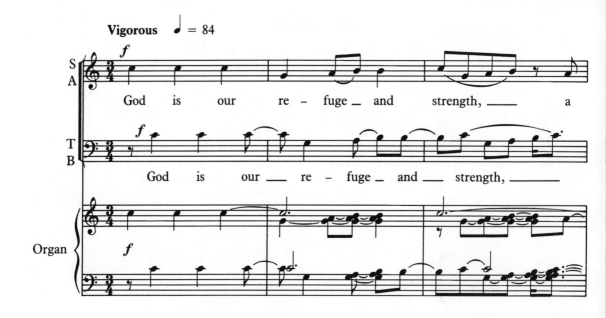

* Lower bass line ad lib.

4

car - ried   in - to the midst of the _ sea; _____

be   carried   in - to the midst of   the   sea; _____

Tranquillo

Be   still   and   know   that

Be   still   and   know   that

Tempo I

I   am   God.   Though the   wa - ters thereof roar ____

I   am   God.   Though   the wa - ters thereof roar ____

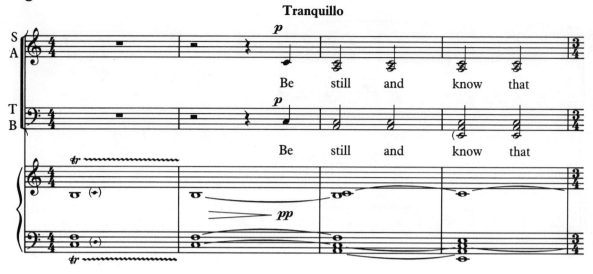

the ho - ly place of the ta - ber - na - cles of the most High.

God is in the midst of her; she shall not be

moved: God shall help her, and that right ear - ly.

8

Tranquillo

S: Be still and know that I am God.

A: Be still and know that I am God.

T: Be still and know that I am God.

B: Be still and know that I am God.

Tempo I

S: The hea- then raged, the

A: The hea- then raged, the

T: The hea- then raged, the

B: The hea- then raged, the